Picture Dictionary!

By J. Douglas Lee

Pictures by David Mostyn

umbrella

Gareth Stevens Publishing
Milwaukee

BRIGHT IDEA BOOKS:

First Words!
Picture Dictionary!
Opposites!
Sounds!

The Four Seasons!
Pets and Animal Friends!
The Age of Dinosaurs!
Baby Animals!

Mouse Count!
Time!
Animal 1*2*3!
Animal ABC!

Homes Then and Now!
Other People, Other Homes!

Library of Congress Cataloging-in-Publication Data

Lee, J. Douglas.
  Picture dictionary!

  (Bright idea books)
  Bibliography: p.
  Summary: Introduces the concept and uses of a dictionary. Special activities explore such dictionary techniques as cross-referring and the grouping of words with similar meanings.
  1. Picture dictionaries, English — Juvenile literature. 2. English language — Alphabet — Juvenile literature. [1. Picture dictionaries] I. Mostyn, David, ill. II. Title.
PE1629.L43   1985   423'.1   85-25135
ISBN O-918831-88-1
ISBN O-918831-87-3 (lib. bdg.)

This North American edition first published in 1985 by

Gareth Stevens, Inc.
7221 West Green Tree Road   Milwaukee, WI 53223, USA

U.S. edition, this format, copyright © 1985
Supplementary text copyright © 1985 by Gareth Stevens, Inc.
Illustrations copyright © 1980 by Octopus Books Limited

First published in the United Kingdom with an original text copyright by Octopus Books Limited.

Typeset by Ries Graphics Ltd.
Series Editors: MaryLee Knowlton and Mark J. Sachner
Cover Design: Gary Moseley
Reading Consultant: Kathleen A. Brau

Contents

Look It Up!: Something to Get the Reader Started

A dictionary can help children learn many things about the words they use every day. It can also help them learn about words they don't use very often — or that they don't use at all!

One of the most helpful things a dictionary does is give young readers an idea of words they can use to mean the same thing or very similar things. Even in a Picture Dictionary like this one, children can find many words that mean the exact same thing, or very close to the same thing.

The step-by-step exercises that follow will help make young readers more familiar with their Picture Dictionary. Just follow the steps below and on the next page one at a time, and see how much this Picture Dictionary can show children about words — and about itself!

These steps are addressed directly to this book's young readers. Grown-ups are encouraged, however, to read the instructions aloud and to guide children through the steps.

1. Have you ever heard the word <u>yacht</u>? (Here's how to say it: <u>yaht</u>.) Do you know what a <u>yacht</u> is? If not, you can find out by looking it up in this book.

2. Look up the word <u>yacht</u> in this book. Now use the picture to help you think of another word that means the same thing as <u>yacht</u>.

3. Can you find that word in this dictionary? Look it up!

4. Now try to use both words in the same sentence.

5. Now let's have some fun and try the same thing with some more words. Look up these words in this book, and see if you can find another word for each: *<u>eagle</u>, *<u>jet</u>, *<u>kitten</u>, *<u>ostrich</u>, *<u>panda</u>, *<u>puppy</u>, *<u>rose</u>, *<u>submarine</u>, and *<u>watch</u>.

6. Congratulations! You have used the dictionary to learn some things about words — and about your dictionary! How did you do?

For more things to do with this Picture Dictionary, look at page 46.

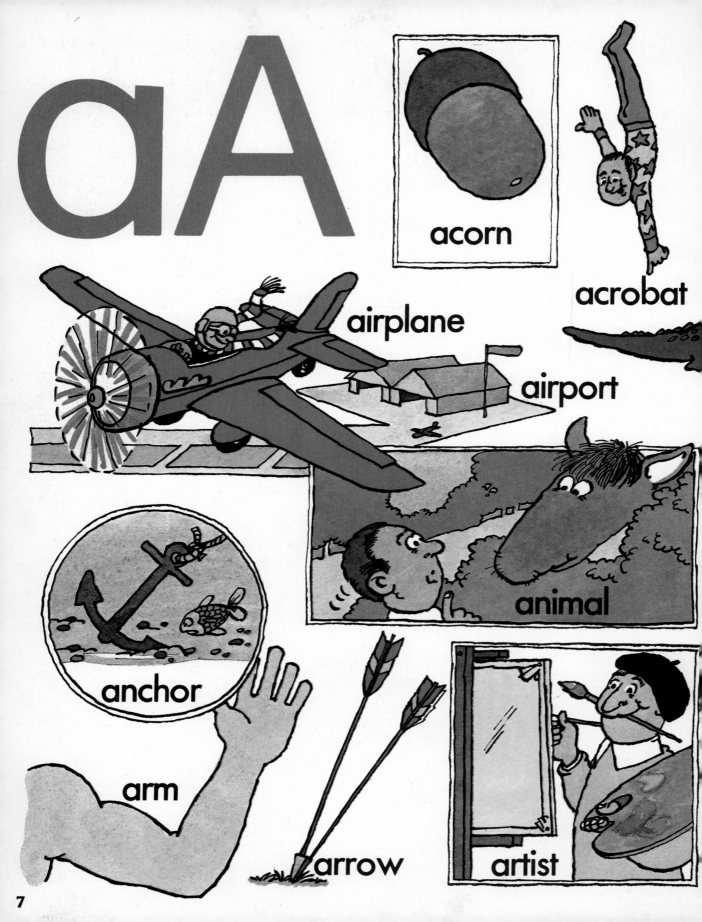

aA

acorn

acrobat

airplane

airport

animal

anchor

arm

arrow

artist

7

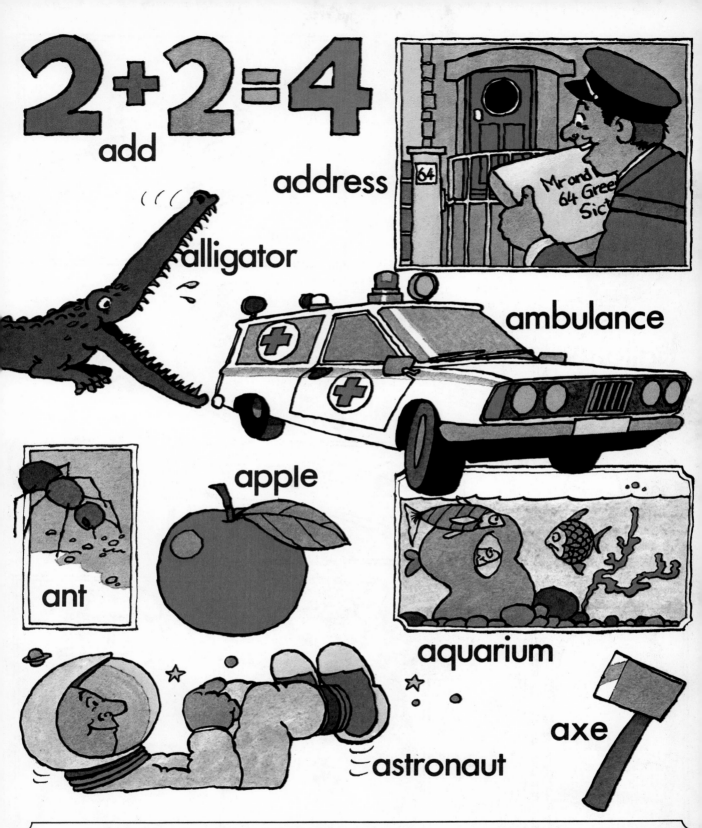

2+2=4
add

address

alligator

ambulance

apple

ant

aquarium

astronaut

axe

a b c d e f g h i j k l m n o p q r s t u v w x y z
A B C D E F G H I J K L M N O P Q R S T U V W X Y Z

bB

baby

ballerina

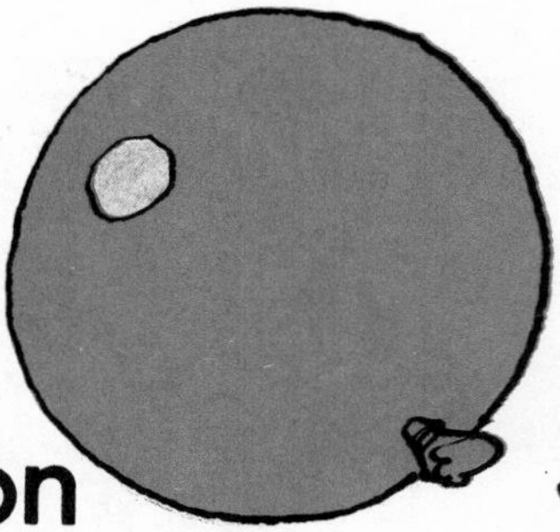

ball

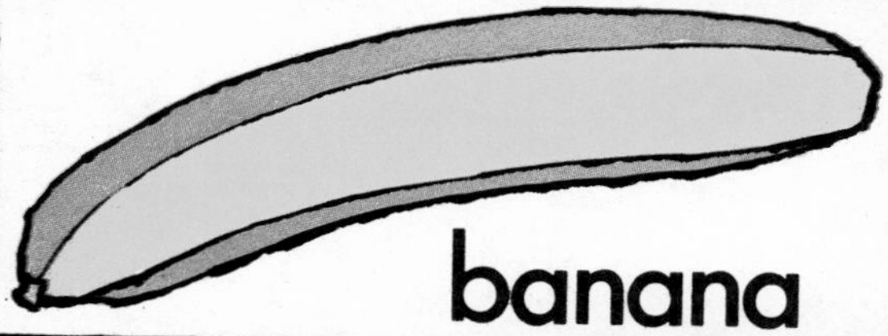

balloon

banana

bark

beads

beak

bear

beard

badge

bag

baker

barrel

basket

bath

bed

bee

bell

bicycle

a **b** c d e f g h i j k l m n o p q r s t u v w x y z
A **B** C D E F G H I J K L M N O P Q R S T U V W X Y Z

9

bB

bird

birthday

book

bottle

box

boy

butcher

bus

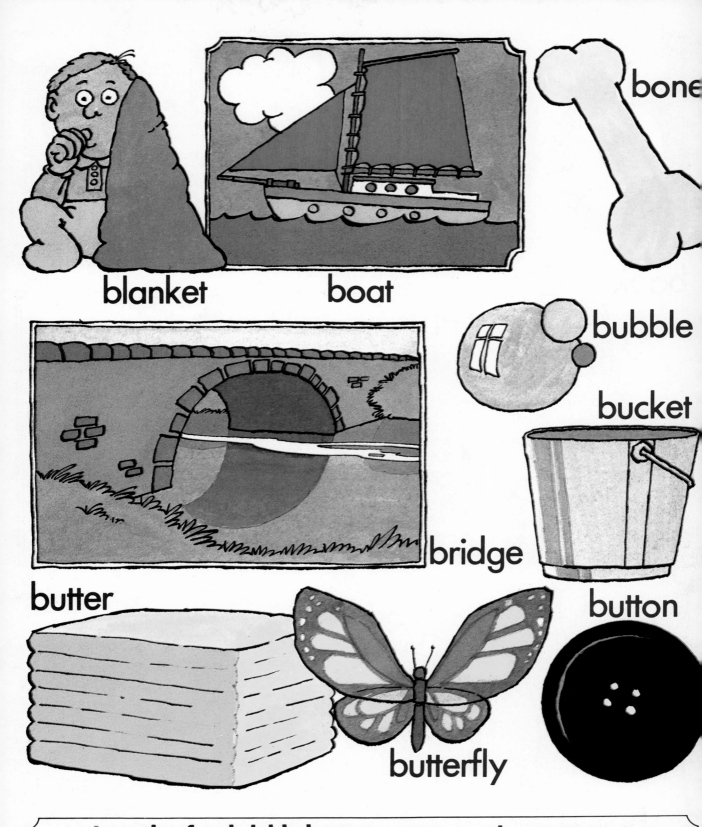

blanket

boat

bone

bubble

bridge

bucket

butter

butterfly

button

a b c d e f g h i j k l m n o p q r s t u v w x y z
A B C D E F G H I J K L M N O P Q R S T U V W X Y Z

11

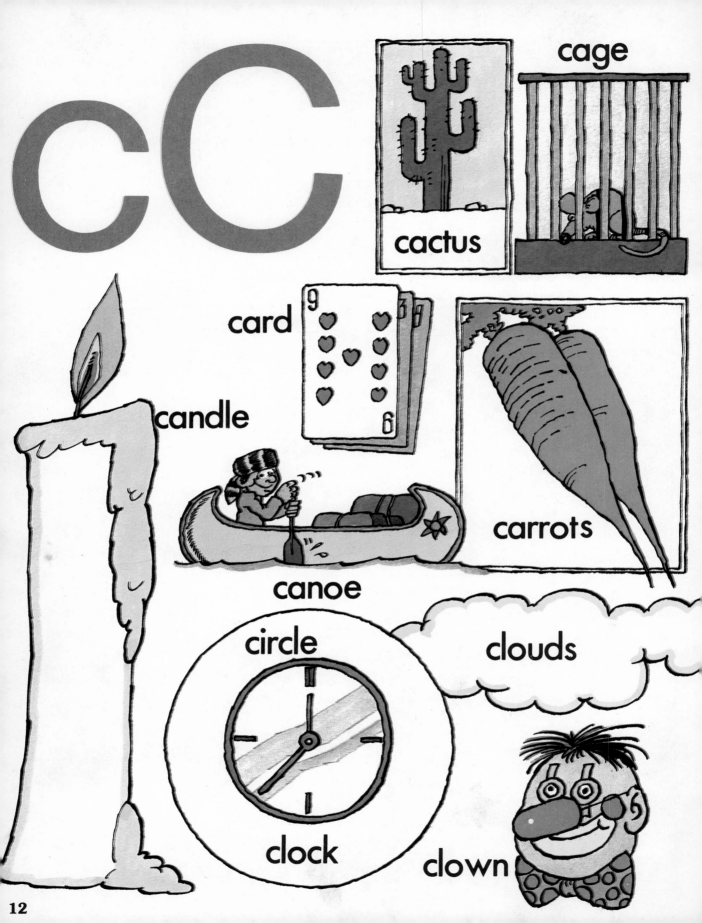

cC

cactus

cage

card

candle

canoe

carrots

circle

clouds

clock

clown

12

cake

camera

camel

castle

cat

chair

chimpanzee

cottage

crab

crane

cup

a b c d e f g h i j k l m n o p q r s t u v w x y z
A B C D E F G H I J K L M N O P Q R S T U V W X Y Z

13

dD

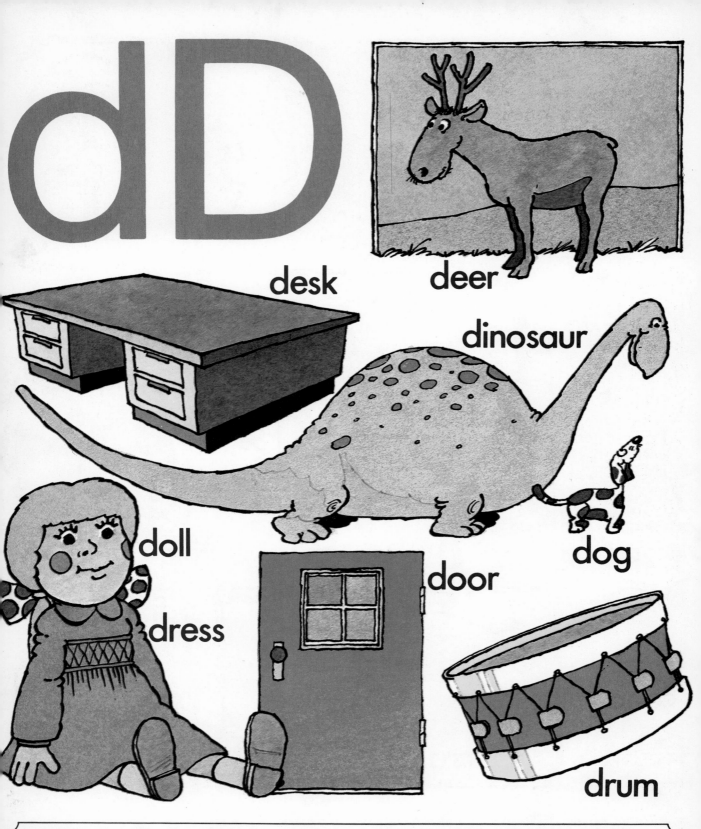

deer

desk

dinosaur

doll

dog

dress

door

drum

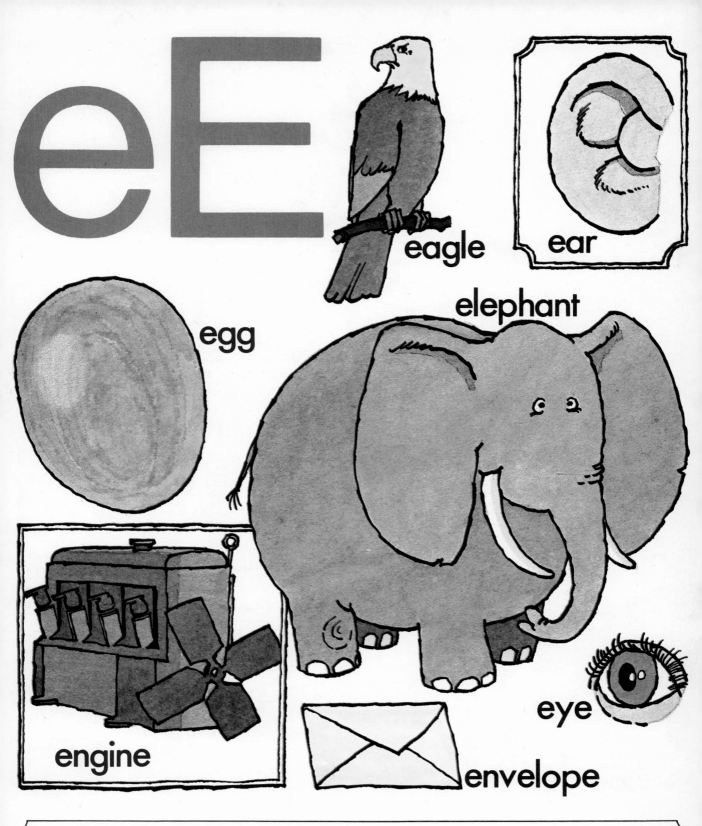

e E

eagle

ear

egg

elephant

engine

envelope

eye

a b c d **e** f g h i j k l m n o p q r s t u v w x y z
A B C D **E** F G H I J K L M N O P Q R S T U V W X Y Z

fF

face

fairy

fence

feather

finger

fireworks

fork

flag

fox

frog

a b c d e f g h i j k l m n o p q r s t u v w x y z
A B C D E F G H I J K L M N O P Q R S T U V W X Y Z

16

gG

giraffe

giant

ghost

glass

glove

guitar

gun

abcdef**g**hijklmnopqrstuvwxyz

ABCDEF**G**HIJKLMNOPQRSTUVWXYZ

hH

hair

hammer

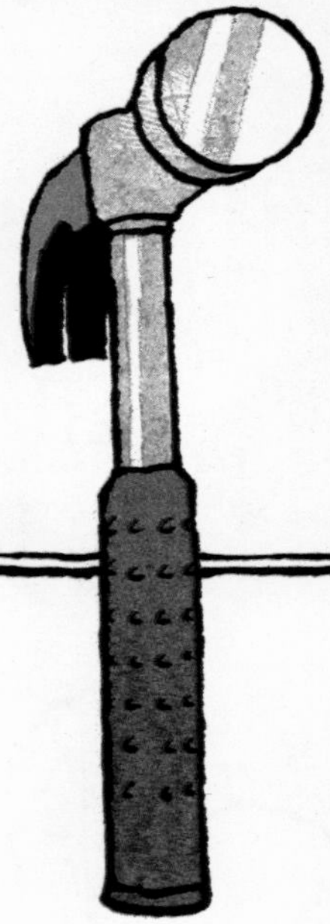

harbor

hat

heart

hippopotamus

hook

horn

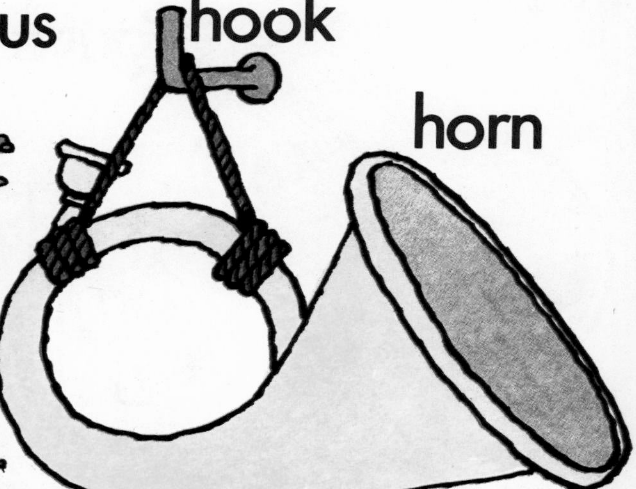

hill

hamster

hand

handkerchief

helicopter

helmet

hen

horse

house

hose

a b c d e f g h i j k l m n o p q r s t u v w x y z

A B C D E F G H I J K L M N O P Q R S T U V W X Y Z

19

Ii

ice cream

igloo

ink

island

iron

abcdefghijklmnopqrstuvwxyz
ABCDEFGHIJKLMNOPQRSTUVWXYZ

20

jJ

jacket

jar

jello

jeans

jet

jungle

abcdefghi**j**klmnopqrstuvwxyz
ABCDEFGHI**J**KLMNOPQRSTUVWXYZ

21

kK

kangaroo

kettle

key

king

kite

kitten

knife

knot

Ll

ladder

leaf

lemon

lightning

lighthouse

lion

lobster

a b c d e f g h i j k l m n o p q r s t u v w x y z
A B C D E F G H I J K L M N O P Q R S T U V W X Y Z

23

mM

machine

map

mask

marbles

medal

milk

magician

mailman

matches

moon

mouse

mug

abcdef ghijkl **m** nopqrstuvwxyz
ABCDEFGHIJKL**M**NOPQRSTUVWXYZ

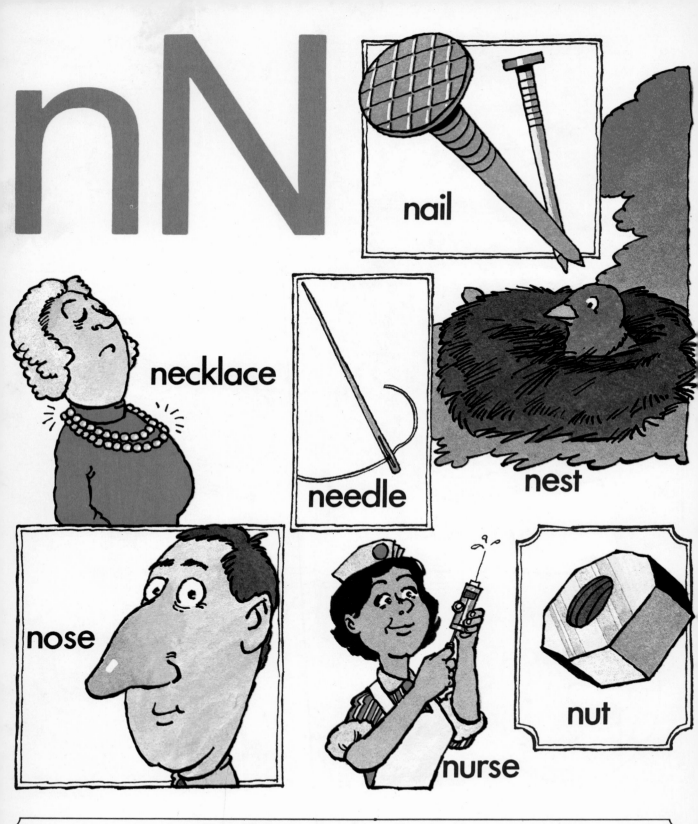

nN

nail

necklace

needle

nest

nose

nurse

nut

Oo

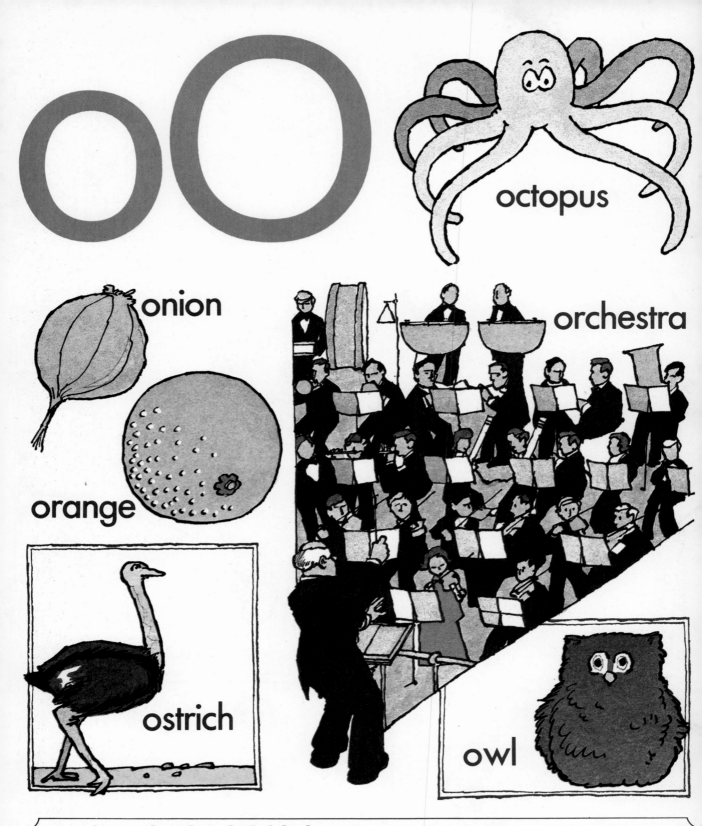

octopus

onion

orange

orchestra

ostrich

owl

abcdefghijklmnopqrstuvwxyz
ABCDEFGHIJKLMNOPQRSTUVWXYZ

pP

paint

patchwork

parrot

photograph

parachute

palace

palm

panda

paw

peacock

pedal

pencil

piano

pie

pig

a b c d e f g h i j k l m n o p q r s t u v w x y z
A B C D E F G H I J K L M N O P Q R S T U V W X Y Z

29

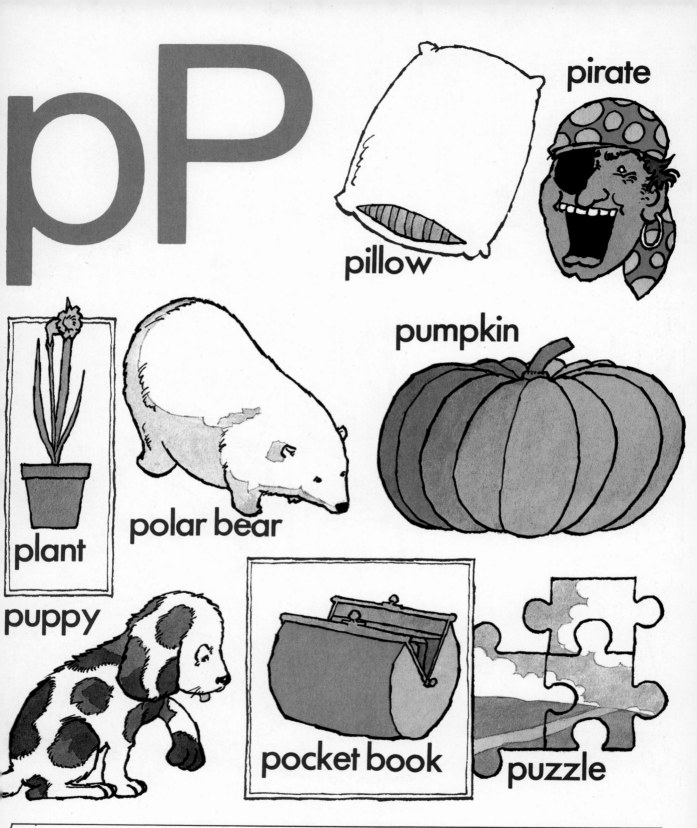

pP

pillow

pirate

pumpkin

plant

polar bear

puppy

pocket book

puzzle

a b c d e f g h i j k l m n o p q r s t u v w x y z
A B C D E F G H I J K L M N O P Q R S T U V W X Y Z

qQ

queen

quiz

quilt

abcdefghijklmnopqrstuvwxyz

ABCDEFGHIJKLMNOPQRSTUVWXYZ

rR

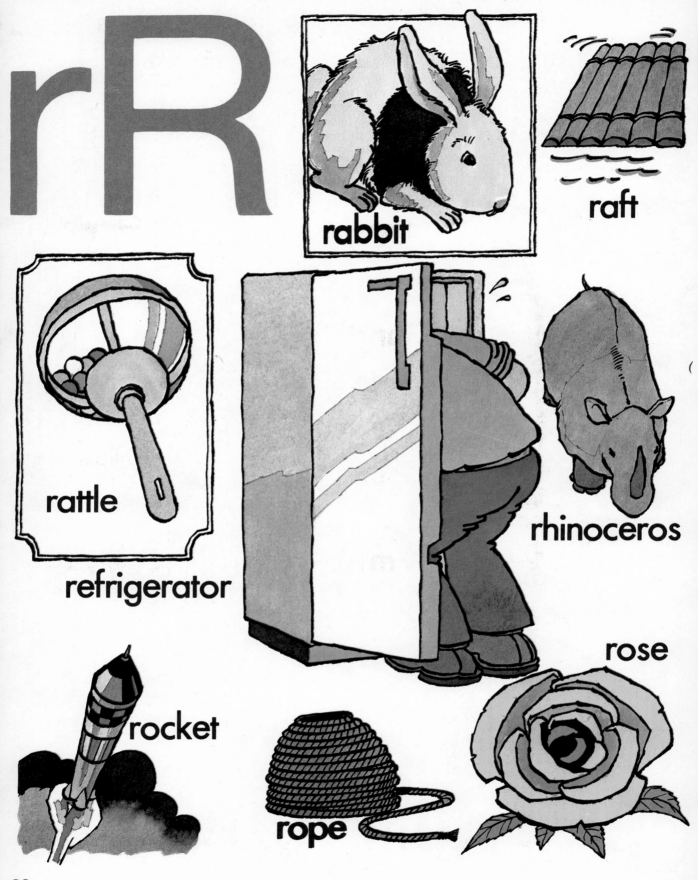

rabbit

raft

rattle

refrigerator

rhinoceros

rocket

rope

rose

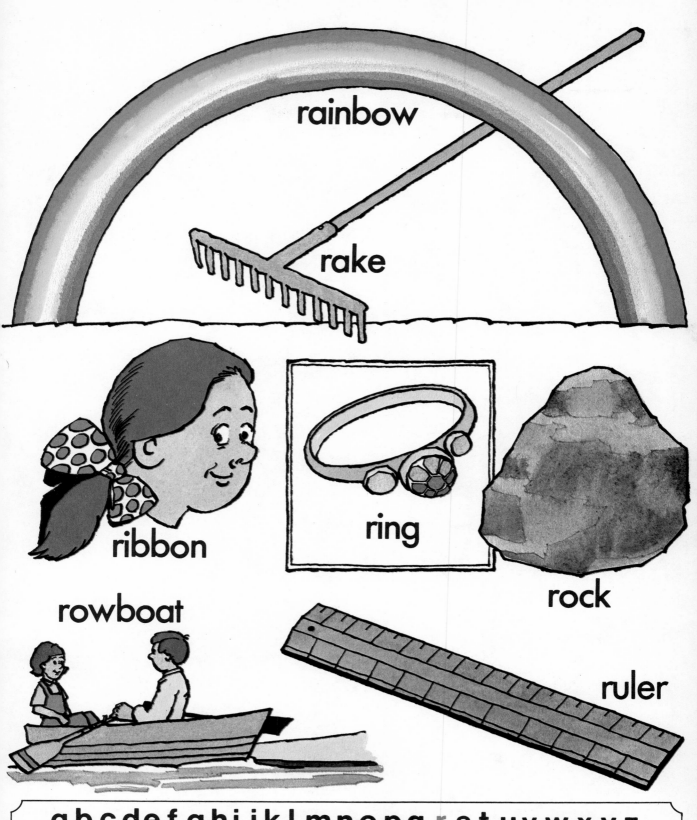

rainbow

rake

ribbon

ring

rock

rowboat

ruler

a b c d e f g h i j k l m n o p q r s t u v w x y z
A B C D E F G H I J K L M N O P Q R S T U V W X Y Z

33

sS

sack

sail

seal

seesaw

skates

skeleton

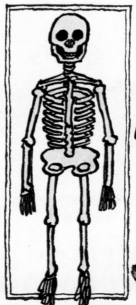

ski

sausage

saw

scissors

shadow

shell

shirt

sled

slide

Ss

snake

snowman

soldier

spoon

sock

stamp

9 pfs

star

submarine

sun

abcdef ghijklmnopqr**s**tuvwxyz
ABCDEFGHIJKLMNOPQR**S**TUVWXYZ

tT

table

tail

taxi

teacher

teddy bear

telephone

television

tent

a b c d e f g h i j k l m n o p q r s t u v w x y z
A B C D E F G H I J K L M N O P Q R S T U V W X Y Z

tT

throne

tie

top

treasure

telescope

toy

tree

tugboat

38

tiger

tomato

tooth

tractor

trampoline

tire

tunnel

typewriter

a b c d e f g h i j k l m n o p q r s **t** u v w x y z
A B C D E F G H I J K L M N O P Q R S **T** U V W X Y Z

39

uU

umbrella

uncle

unicorn

uniform

abcdefghijklmnopqrstuvwxyz
ABCDEFGHIJKLMNOPQRSTUVWXYZ

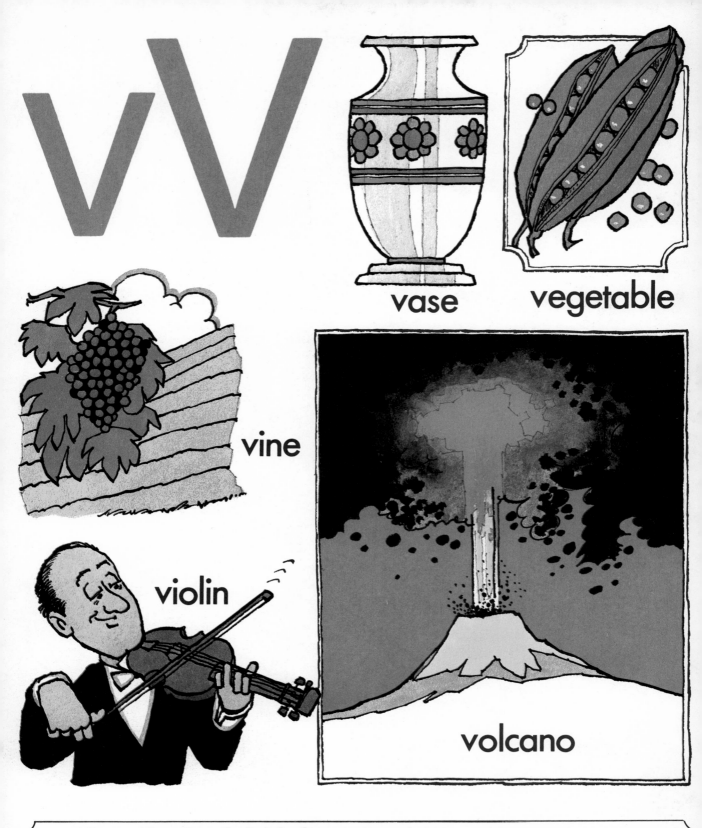

vV

vase

vegetable

vine

violin

volcano

wW

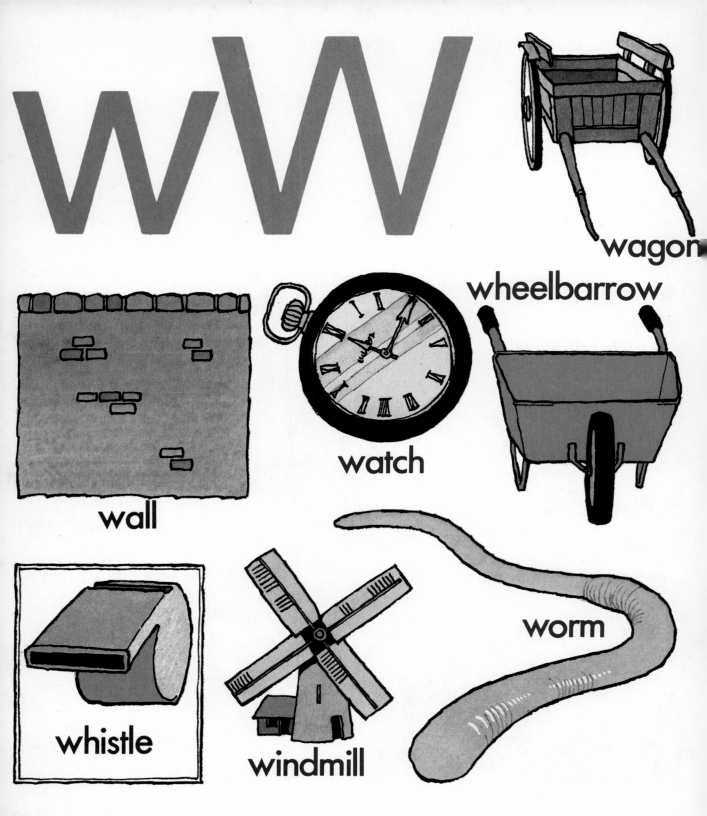

wagon

wheelbarrow

wall

watch

worm

whistle

windmill

abcdefghijklmnopqrstuvwxyz

ABCDEFGHIJKLMNOPQRSTUVWXYZ

42

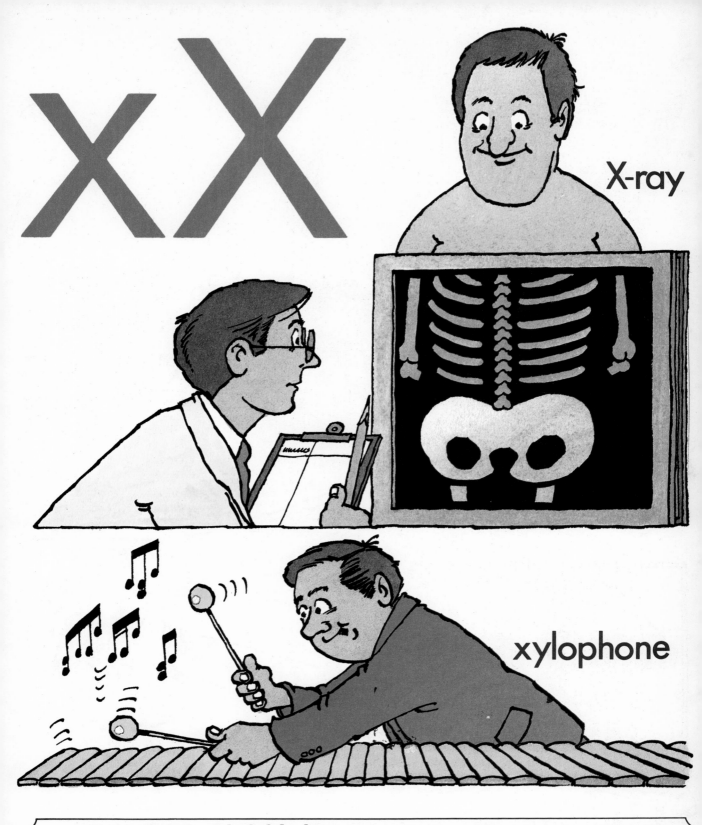

xX

X-ray

xylophone

abcdefghijklmnopqrstuvw**x**yz
ABCDEFGHIJKLMNOPQRSTUVW**X**YZ

43

yY

yacht

yarn

yoga

yo yo

abcdefghijklmnopqrstuvwxy**z**
ABCDEFGHIJKLMNOPQRSTUVWX**YZ**

44

Zz

zebra

zigzag

zipper

zoo

abcdefghijklmnopqrstuvwxyz
ABCDEFGHIJKLMNOPQRSTUVWXYZ

45

Things to Talk About and Do

Like the "Look It Up!" exercises on pages 4-5, the
following "Things to Talk About and Do" offer grown-
ups suggestions for further ideas and activities to share
with young readers of Picture Dictionary!

1. You can find the word dog in this book. What sound
   does a dog make? Can you find the word for this
   sound in the book? Look it up!

2. Here are some more words you can find in this
   book. Find the picture for each word in the list:
   *magician, *X-ray, *artist.

   Can you talk about what you see in each picture?

3. Look at the words for the letters S and T on pages
   36 and 37. Can you use each word in its own
   sentence?

4. Look up the word map in your Picture Dictionary.
   How many things in the picture can you name?
   Write them on a piece of paper, or find a grown-up
   to help you write them. Now see how many of these
   words you can find in this dictionary.

More Books About Words

Here are some more books about words. Look at the list. If you see any books you would like to read, see if your library or bookstore has them.

ABC of Children's Names. Ewen (Green Tiger Press)
All Butterflies: An ABC. Brown (Atheneum)
Animal ABC! Lee (Gareth Stevens)
Animal 1*2*3! Lee (Gareth Stevens)
Big and Little. Weigle (Grosset & Dunlap)
Dr. Seuss's ABC Soup. Dr. Seuss (Random House)
Eight Ate: A Feast of Homonym Riddles. Terban
    (Houghton Mifflin)
Fast-Slow, High-Low: A Book of Opposites. Spier
    (Doubleday)
First Words! Lee (Gareth Stevens)
Guinea Pig ABC. Duke (Dial)
High Sounds, Low Sounds. Branley (Harcourt Brace
    Jovanovich)
How to Write Codes and Send Secret Messages.
    Peterson (Scholastic Book Service)
Little Monster's Alphabet Book. Mayer (Golden Press)
Max's First Word. Wells (Dial)
My Word Book. Grosset & Dunlap (Grosset & Dunlap)
Opposites! Lee (Gareth Stevens)
A Phenomenal Alphabet Book. Edens (Green Tiger
    Press)
Secrets with Ciphers and Codes. Rothman (Macmillan)
Sesame Street Sign Language Fun. Bove (Random
    House/Children's Television Workshop)
*Simon & Schuster's Illustrated Young Reader's
    Dictionary* (Simon & Schuster)
Sounds! Lee (Gareth Stevens)
Traffic: A Book of Opposites. Maestro (Crown)
What's That You Said?: How Words Change. Weiss
    (Harcourt Brace Jovanovich)
When Will I Read? Cohen (Dell)
Word Works: Why the Alphabet Is a Kid's Best Friend.
    Kaye (Little, Brown)

For Grown-ups

Picture Dictionary! is a picture book that uses simple words and clever illustrations to reinforce children's ABCs and introduce them to the concept — and use — of a dictionary. The controlled vocabulary text (pages 6-45) complements and challenges a young reader's developing language and reading skills. Of particular value is a "Something to Get the Reader Started" section that provides an enjoyable, yet challenging, series of steps that introduce young readers to such dictionary techniques as cross-referring and grouping words with similar meanings.

The editors invite interested adults to examine the grade level estimate at the bottom of this page. Certain books lend themselves to reading analyses using standard reading tests. *Picture Dictionary!,* because of its format, does not. This concept book helps children discriminate among objects by size, color, shape, and placement within the alphabet. The reading level of *Picture Dictionary!* is therefore determined not only by how "hard" the words are, but by a child's ability to grasp the subject matter in a visual format.

The grade level given below reflects our critical judgment about the appropriate level at which children find the subject matter an achievable challenge.

Estimated reading level: Grade level 1-3